The Frugal Fac

Better Living through Rebates, Discount and Deals.

Strategies to keep money in **your** pocket.

www.TheFrugalFactor.com

ISBN-13: 978-0-9820631-0-1   ISBN-10: 0-9820631-0-5

Publication Data
Scime', Paul.
The Frugal Factor: Better living through Rebates Discounts and Deals.
    Includes index
    ISBN 0-9820631-0-5
    1. Reference: Consumer Guides 2. Personal Finance - Budgeting
    I. Title

The publisher and the author make no representation or warranties with respect to the accuracy or completeness of the contents of this work and specifically disclaim all warranties, including without limitation warranties of fitness for a particular purpose. The advice and strategies contained herein may not be suitable for every situation. This work is sold with the understanding that the publisher is not engaged in rendering legal, accounting, or other professional services. The fact that an organization or website is referred to in this work as a citation and or potential source of further information does not mean that the author or publisher endorses the information the organization or website may provide or recommendations it may make. Further readers should be aware that Internet websites listed in this work may have changed or disappeared between when this work was written and when it is read.

Store and product names mention in this book are trademarks of their perspective companies. Extrabucks is a trademark of CVS Caremark Corporation, Centurion is a trademark of American Express, Easyrebates is a trademark of Staples, Inc., M&M's is a trademark of Mars incorporated.

This book is available at a special discount when purchased in bulk for premium and sales promotions as well as fund raising and educational use. For information contact the publisher: Prime Technology Corporation, P.O. Box 784501, Winter Garden, Florida 34778

About the Author

Paul Scime' has been a high school teacher for over twenty years in Orlando, Florida. He has previously authored software and texts on a variety of subjects including Digital Electronics, Fiber Optics and Applied Mathematics. His obsession with rebates and free items started in the 1980's when extra computer mice, keyboards and floppy disks were needed for his classroom. Over the years this hobby of getting items at a reduced cost, and at times FREE has expanded to Internet deals, grocery coupons, rebates and more!

Frugal - Economical in use or expenditure; prudently saving or sparing; not wasteful.

Factor - One of the elements contributing to a particular result or situation.

The words in the title of this book provide its objective. To teach you the skills and strategies that result in saving money and improving your lifestyle.

Code 1231

Special Thanks:

To my Mom and Dad, for without their guidance and
friendship, I would truly be lost.

And

To my wife and kids who have endured all these deals!

"Do the Deal !"

Contents

Introduction

I am crazy for rebates and coupons. I have saved and made thousands of dollars using rebate and coupon offers. It's a great way to get products cheap, for FREE or even make money.

Living a frugal life is more than just using coupons and rebates; it's about making well-informed choices. It means living below your means without suffering or doing without. You can do this by learning how to use research to find the best product and best deals on all types of products from items in grocery stores, to computers, to cars and more.

Learning to live a Frugal life will allow you to control your money and lifestyle, instead of it controlling you.

Saving money and shopping well can be a challenging hobby and an educational experience for you and your children. It can even turn into a sport when you involve your entire family. The following pages will provide you with information and resources to get more for your money, and have fun while doing it. As you read I hope you find new frugal ideas and revisit some you already knew.

Remember:

It's not how much money you make; it's how much you keep!

1

Rebates

While popular with manufacturers, consumers have had a love/hate relationship with rebates over the years. The following pages will help make your rebates a profitable and rewarding experience.

Rebates

Rebates began in the 1970's when companies like Proctor and Gamble used rebates to advertise small discounts without actually changing the price of the product. The popularity of rebates exploded in the 1990's when computer makers, cell phone and other high technology companies used rebates as a way of moving large piles of high tech equipment that were becoming obsolete.

The use of rebates increased the volume of sales beyond the expectations of the manufacturers. Along with this increase in sales came a large increase in the number of rebates being submitted. As a result some manufacturers were overwhelmed and many rebates went unfilled. Protest from consumers brought about many changes and the creation of "fulfillment" companies to handle the rebates and mailing of the checks.

Due to massive complaints in the late 90's (from unfulfilled and invalid rebates), many retail stores now offer online rebate submissions. This process has provided better customer service and reduced the number of fraudulent rebate submissions.

The online submission process has reduced customer wait time (the time needed for the rebate check to arrive), and also reduced breakage. Any time someone buys a rebate-eligible offering, but fails to get the money, is what the industry calls "breakage." Believe it or not some consumers never cash their rebates checks. The industry calls this "Slippage".

Sometimes consumers attempt to submit bogus rebates. Fraudulent rebate submissions have become such a problem that one retailer has over 12,000 addresses on a watch list for fraudulent rebate submissions.

Many people will not be bothered filling out rebates and find it a difficult and frustrating task. Have you ever been in a store and purchased an item with a rebate. Before buying the item, you convinced yourself that you would complete and mail in the rebate. But when you arrived home it was quickly forgotten, or just something you never got around to. Well that happens everyday around the country. When that happens the store and manufactures win, and you lose.

Visit TheFrugalFactor.com and enter the code below for additional information.

Code 599

How rebates work

The manufacturer, the retail store, or both can offer a rebate. Most often the rebate is mailed. You purchase the product and apply for your rebate by using the rebate form and mailing it to the rebate submission center.

A retailer can offer a rebate to make the product seem cheaper. An example of this can be found in the newspaper every Sunday. An advertisement showing a laser printer for only $39.99 and in small print it states "after $90 rebate". That advertisement was actually in my Sunday paper, and I bought the printer. The product was a Samsung laser printer. I paid $129.99 for the printer. I filled out the rebate form and sent it in with a copy of my receipt. In about eight weeks I received a check for $90.00. This means $129.99 − 90.00 - $39.99. Great Deal, Great Printer! This deal turned out to be a great price on a wonderful product.

You are more likely to buy the $39.99 product over the $129.99 product. The customer's perception is that the price is cheaper.

It seems cheaper, and is, <u>if you follow through and complete the rebate</u>. You will buy it, mail in the rebate form, and get a certain amount back after an 8 to 12 week delay. But after the purchase, many people never get around to filling out the rebate and mailing it in. Many who mail in the rebate don't follow the instructions; therefore the rebate is never fulfilled or must be resubmitted.

Companies make large profits from customers who buy the product but then fail to send for the rebate. One rebate fulfillment company estimated a 10% redemption rate for a $10 rebate on a $100 product, and a 35% redemption rate on a $200 product with a $50 rebate.

I once read that Staples and its vendors pay out over 3.5 million dollars a week in rebates. Now that is a staggering number. These are from the people, who send in the rebate, think about the people who never applied for their rebate.

For pictures of deals mentioned in this book visit:

TheFrugalFactor.com

The Submission

Rebates: I love 'em; I hate 'em; I can't live without them! Remember that stores and manufacturers do not usually fulfill their own rebates. They hire rebate fulfillment houses to do that. Sometimes it seems like they count on you forgetting to send in the rebate, filling out the form wrong, mailing it in late, or forgetting to include the UPC barcode, serial number, or other requested item.

When filling out your rebate remember these 10 rules:

1. Only buy a product if your OK with paying full price.

2. Only buy from manufacturers, or stores you trust. If the rebate exceeds $100 your might think about mailing it certified return receipt requested, and keep the receipt when it is returned to you.

3. Check the rebate dates and mailing dates before you decide to purchase.

4. Get all forms before leaving the store. If the deal is online, print the forms before placing your order.

5. Read the fine print and obey all the rules. Be sure to include all the requested information. Circle the rebate item and its price on the receipt. Provide only the required information, the original receipt & UPC if requested. If they only want a copy, then send only a copy of the UPC and receipt. There

may be another rebate for the same item that requires the original UPC symbol.

The serial number is commonly requested for computers, printers and digital cameras. This may be on a sticker on the outside of the box, next to the UPC code, and on the actual product.

6. Don't discard the box until you have completed the rebate. If you forget you may be digging through the trash for that UPC barcode. Several times I have had to run down to the curb in the middle of the night to cut a UPC code off a box!

7. Some rebates are not worth the time. Set your own threshold. For me any rebate $5 or less is not worth the time and frustration of filling out the rebate form. Also, most rebates require the expense of a stamp and envelope.

8. Follow up on any rebate that is more than 12 weeks old. This is done by visiting the website listed on the rebate, or calling a toll free number that is usually on the rebate form.

9. Fill out the rebate by hand, using your neatest handwriting. Filling out the rebate by hand is a requirement of many rebates. In order to make the fulfillment company's job easier, I also stick a label on the rebate form that has my mailing address on it. This makes it easy for them to read.

10. Be sure to keep a copy of everything you send. Repeat – be sure to keep a copy of everything you send.

The Resubmit

Sometimes you will get a post card stating that your rebate is invalid. This is a common method used by the fulfillment houses. You can call them or resubmit your rebate by mail. When resubmitting a rebate, highlight all of the information that the postcard or letter stated was missing. Send a copy of everything that you sent the first time, including a copy of the post card or letter that was sent stating that your rebate was invalid. Many times a phone call will get your rebate validated.

Read-Read-Read

Be sure to print and read the rebate form. Most rebates are one per person, household or organization. This means you can get only one rebate! If you have a friend or family member that will allow you to use their address you may be able to get an additional rebate offer. The problem with that is your friend or family member might also want the deal!

Read the rebate form carefully, some only allow one rebate, per person, per year. This often happens with some anti-virus software programs. Your rebate may be denied since you already received a rebate during the rebate period.

All hope is not lost! There are times when it's allowed to get more than one product per rebate. Sometimes the limit is three, ten or even more. One rather famous multiple rebate offer is from Staples. About once a year Staples offers battery operated pencil sharpeners FAR (Free after Rebate). The limit is 10 per person per household.

You guessed right. Each year I purchase 10 pencil sharpeners. You might wonder what I do with all those pencil sharpeners. Remember that I am a teacher so, most of these are given away to students at my school.

The Double Dip

The double dip is when a store and a manufacturer offer a rebate at the same time, on the same item. Most of the time these rebates will only overlap by a day or two.

Warning: You many not qualify for both rebates, because they may both request the original UPC. If you are lucky there are a few items that have two UPC symbols (this happens on some large items like office chairs). If the store you are purchasing the item from also uses an online rebate system that does not require the UPC symbol, you may be able to get both rebates.

Be aware that some stores show a rebate that is actually the manufacturer's rebate. Check the mailing address or department number to see if they are the same. If they are the same you will not be able to double dip. In reality the store is just processing the manufacturers rebate. So, you won't get both.

Usually the retailer does not know about, or advertise the second manufacturer's rebate. Check the manufacturer's web site, or the "Deal" sites for these offers. Occasionally stores will offer 2 rebates. One is good for only one day (like Black Friday) and the other is good all week.

At times you can use several offers to get an item for less than Free. Officemax had a promotion that gave a $30 gift card with the purchase of selected printers. One of the printers was a Brother laser printer that had a manufacturer's rebate. Plus, if I paid with Paypal, I would receive a 25% rebate directly to my

Paypal account. After it was all over I profited by about $21 dollars, and shipping for the printer was free.

The Peel

Also, I recommend peeling the UPC symbol off the package without going all the way through the box. Use a razor blade to cut only through the first layer of the box to remove the UPC symbol. By keeping the UPC symbol thin it will go through the U.S. postal service sorting equipment easier.

Hey, remember the faster it gets to the rebate Fulfillment Company the faster you will get your rebate check. This method is also an advantage when the Ebay factor comes into play.

The Record

Always keep a copy of everything you send to the rebate fulfillment house. Use a file folder or three ring binder and keep the copies in order by date. When the rebate check arrives, you can discard the copies of the rebates.

Also, check your folder for any rebates that are over 12 weeks. If you have not received the rebate in 12 weeks, it's time to call the fulfillment company and ask what happened to your check.

When a check comes in, it should be for the oldest rebate. If there are older rebates in your book, it may be time to check their status by looking them up online, or giving the fulfillment company a call. This information is on the rebate form.

The rebate fulfillment companies sometimes have problems with volume, and may delay sending out your rebate. Many send out Visa Debit cards instead of a check. Creating these cards sometimes causes a delay. Also, the rebate fulfillment company can only pay the rebate, when the company it represents releases the funds to pay the rebates. A few years back, I had a $40 Linens & Things rebate that took 10 months to receive. It finally arrived after four phone calls. When I called the rebate fulfillment company they were polite and stated my rebate was ready to go, and all they needed was to have the funds released by Linens & Things. The fourth call was direct to Linens & Things corporate office. As, you may know Linens & Things was having problems and went out of business in 2009.

Online Rebates

These are the best! The online rebates are fulfilled faster for the customer and reduce fraud for the product companies. Online rebates became very popular at Staples.com. Using your store receipt, or the order confirmation e-mail, you enter the receipt number, the order number, and the products that are entitled to a rebate.

No stamp, No UPC needed!

In a few weeks your rebate will arrive!

My Staples "Easyrebates" arrive faster than any others.

Rebate Tracking

When a rebate reaches the 12-week, mark and the check has not arrived, it's time to track down your check. Before calling about a rebate visit the web site listed on the rebate form. This may give you your answer about the rebate, it is much faster and you will not spend any time on hold waiting for a CSR (Customer Service Representative).

If the rebate does not appear on the site, make the phone call. If the rebate shows that the check was mailed and more than ten days have passed, its time to make the call. Over the years I have a few rebates that were lost in the mail. The checks were never cashed and the rebate fulfillment company sent a new check.

The Payment

Fraud is a major problem that the rebate fulfillment houses are fighting. To aid in this fight, many are now sending the rebates in the form of debit cards or gift cards. Some stores, like Walgreen's will actually increase the amount of your rebate by 10% if you will accept the rebate in the form of a store gift card. A few are even sending the rebate money using Paypal.

The annoying thing about Visa debit cards is that you have to spend <u>exactly the amount on the card</u> to get all the money out, if you spend over the amount on the card it will be rejected.

For example: When using a store gift card the entire amount on the card can be used. For example, if you purchase a $23.50 item with a $25 store gift card you will have $1.50 left on the card. You can use that gift card to purchase a $5 item. At the register a $1.50 will be taken from the gift card and you will need to pay the remaining $3.50.

When using a Visa Debit card if you make the same $23.50 purchase, leaving $1.50 on the card, but when you attempt to buy the $5 item the card will be rejected. The card is rejected because there are not enough funds left on the card. If you know the balance on the card you could tell the cashier and she would enter that amount and tell you how much cash you need to complete the purchase.

When you get these Visa debit cards, trade them for store gift cards in the same amount. Then use that card when shopping at the store. This will allow you to use the entire amount!

Otherwise you may leave some money on the rebate's Visa debit card. When you do this, the manufacturer and fulfillment company win again.

Code 125

F.A.R. Factor

F.A.R. (FREE after Rebate): nothing is Free. You must fill out the rebate form, spend your time and effort, and spend the cost of a postage stamp. Now that I have said that, read on.

A very effective strategy is to buy FAR items, to get your total dollar purchase high enough to use a coupon code. For example if a store offers cordless phone for $20, with a $20 rebate and the limit is 10 rebates per person, you have a situation were you can actually make money.

It is very common for a store to have a coupon that provides $20 off $100 purchase, or $30 off $150. By buying five phones and using the $20 off $100 coupon you have already made money. (5 x 20.00 = 100.00 - 20.00 off) pay $80.00. Then send for the $100.00 rebate = $20 profit.

F.A.R. + Code = Profit

You may think that this is never going to happen. I find deals like this happen almost every other month. Each time it happens I think, WOW this will never happen again, but then a month or two later I find the same kind of deal on another product. I always post these deals on TheFrugalFactor.com toolbar when they happen.

Now I do not suggest buying phones that you do not need. But, if there was an item you wanted, you could effectively reduce its price by adding a FAR item and a dollar off coupon. Some stores like Office Depot have major exclusions for using their dollar off coupons. Most technology items can not be combined with an Office Depot dollar off coupon. Office supply and electronics stores need to protect themselves because technology items offer a very small percentage of profit for the store. Read the fine print before using a coupon, or just give it a try.

Another thing to keep in mind is that most stores will honor their competitor's coupons. For example, Staples will honor an Office Depot coupon. So, you receive a coupon in the mail for $30 off $150 you may be able to use it at any retail office supply store.

Time Change

A few years ago the combination of a rebate, and daylight savings time gave me a FREE After Rebate Canon D320 copy machine/laser printer. At the time Office Depot had the machine on sale for $125. The advertisement that started the next Sunday was posted on their website the Friday before. It showed the machine at a price of $249 before a $125 rebate.

I stayed up late Saturday night, into Sunday morning placing my order at around 1 A.M. in the morning. Due to the time change the price on the web site was still $125, but the date on the emailed invoice was Sunday's date. This made the $125 rebate valid. The machine was FREE After Rebate. I only had to pay tax and the cost of the stamp to mail in the rebate.

Needless to say, when the rebate check arrived in my mailbox, I was very happy!

Fulfillment Company Contacts

Below are some of the more popular fulfillment companies and their contact information. For a complete list visit TheFrugalFactor.com

Amazon.com Customer Service
Phone 800-201-7575 Fax 206 266-2950

Continental Promotions Group - www.rebatestatus.com
800-554-9838, 888-314-9908
Fax 480-606-4313

OnRebate - www.onrebate.com
120 East Palmetto Park Road
Boca Raton, FL 33432
888-222-9300

Parago / RebatesHQ – Rebateshq.com 877-580-3348
800-886-8370 (FAX Number)
877-378-8545
Resubmission address:
P.O. BOX 28516
Miami, FL 33102-8516

Young America Fulfillment Center - www.young-america.com
717 Faxon Road
Young America, MN 55397-9481
(952) 467-1100, 952-294-6209

Young America Client Services Facility
18671 Lake Drive East
Chanhassen, MN 55317
(952) 294-6000

www.GFSINC.com
www.web-rebates.com (Main rebate webpage)
240-209-8498 (FAX)
800-477-1626 (FAX resubmissions)

Staples
Coppell, TX & McAllen, TX (Parago / RebatesHQ) & Miami, FL
StaplesRebates.com, www.stapleseasyrebates.com
877-549-9794, 800-338-0252

Walgreen's
www.walgreens.com
Consumer Relations
200 Wilmot Rd.
Deerfield, IL 60015
800-289-2273
847-914-3105 (Fax)

Code 328

2

Online Deals

Some of the best deals are found on the Internet.

No driving to the store.
No fighting the weather.
No dragging your children to the store.
Easy online comparison-shopping.
Shop anytime, day or night.
Shop in your underwear (Did I just say that?)

The Giveaway

Many office supply stores will give away items with orders over a certain dollar amount. For example Office Depot once provided a free CD boom box/AM/FM radio with any order over $150. In order to get the free item you need to know the item number and coupon code. You add the item to your cart and then apply the coupon code to deduct the amount of that item at checkout. You may end up paying tax on the item. The stated retail cost of the radio is $59 or more. Now remember, this is a giveaway item, it's nice, but it is usually not worth $59.

Code 579

Coupon Codes

Online coupon codes are wonderful!

Most coupon codes are for a dollar value off. For example $15 off $75 purchase or $75 off $500 purchase. To get the discount all you need to do is enter the coupon code when going through the checkout process.

Other coupon codes will expire after a certain number of uses. For example Dell.com might provide a coupon code that discounts 1,000 laptop computers. After 1,000 computers are sold using the coupon, the coupon stops working. At times a coupon is so successful the website becomes overwhelmed with traffic.

Some retail web sites allow you to use more than one coupon code at a time. Usually this allows me to use a discount code and free shipping code.

How do you get coupon codes? There are several websites that list coupon codes. Many times coupons codes arrive in the mail printed on post cards or catalogs.

Be aware that on Ebay there are many sellers of coupon codes that can be found for FREE on the Internet.

Check these websites out for coupon codes:

CurrentCodes.com
DealHunting.com
CouponCabin.com
RetailMeNot.com
NaughtyCodes.com
Tjoos.com

Web Only Deals

Due to the high cost of gas, and the fact that I am lazy, I would just rather stay home. I buy as much as possible on the Internet. Usually I can buy online cheaper than visiting the store. Also, many items are shipped free.

Office supply and electronics stores offer web only specials, or simply have lower prices on their web site. So, if you are looking for a computer, printer, or stereo - always check the prices online before you go to the store.

Online sales change very quickly. For example CompUSA had a computer on sale for $199, after a $50 rebate. This was a great deal. This deal started on Sunday. In order to get the deal I would need to be outside the store before it opened, or if the deal was also on their web site I would order online. I located the item on the web site. The computer was still the regular price. A few minutes after midnight I refreshed the screen and the sale price of $199 appeared. I ordered one. I kept watching the site and at 12:23 AM the deal changed, it was then sold out for online orders and available in store only.

Many times I have ordered an item online for in store pickup. Then a few hours later I would check back to find that the product is now only available in store and can no longer be ordered for in store pickup! When a retailer gets hit with massive amounts of sales they can change the availability quickly. Online retailers that also have brick and mortar stores would rather have you physically visit the store. Consumers are more likely to buy additional items (impulse buy) at the store.

Google Froogle

How you arrive at a web site sometimes will determine the price that you pay. I have found that by using Google's Froogle.com web site to search for a product, I may end up with a lower price. This phenomenon is not unique to froogle.com. This is also true when using special promotional links.

There are times when an office supply store will provide special sales. But in order to get the special price you must place the order using the order number only. This is done on the section of the web site that allows you to order by catalog number. The same item can be seen on their site but at over three times the special sale cost.

Many times this information leak is more by design, and not by accident. It gets consumers excited about the purchase!

On Google, Froogle is now called "Shopping".

The Print

If you find a great deal online be sure to print the web page showing the price of the item. I remember buying a gas grill at Homedepot.com. It was, and still is the best grill I have ever owned. The cost was $187 w/tax delivered. It was one of those stainless steel models! They offered free shipping, which must have been an error, because the free shipping lasted only a few hours.

The regular price of the grill at Homedepot.com was $499. What happened? Well my credit card was charged the full $499. Some people were very upset that they were charged the wrong price. Some stated they would file a complaint with the FTC and more... I was not worried. I had my printout of the web page with the stated price and free shipping.

I waited for the grill to be delivered and within a week I received an e-mail apology from HD, it also stated that my credit card would be credited with the $312 overcharge.

It may have been a price error, but I had the printout of the website, showing the price. If Home Depot did not fix the error I would have simply called and requested to return the grill since they did not deliver it at the advertised price. I would, of course, insist that they pick up the grill. I really did not think they would pay the expense of having UPS pick up the grill. Home Depot did the right thing, and made my life easier. Now, everytime I go into a Home Depot store, I have a positive outlook!

Viral marketing – well almost

Viral marketing is an amazing thing. It is a strategy that encourages people to pass on a marketing message to others. This creates the potential for exponential growth. Often called "word of mouth advertising", or "buzz factor" it has launched some products into our common experience. From the Apple Ipod to Pop Rocks, we know what they are because their advertising traveled like a virus.

Viral marketing allows some products to not just identify a product category but become it. My students often call any MP3 player an Ipod. Even though an IPOD is the MP3 player only made by Apple. This shows how effectively Apple markets their products.

Although not true viral marketing, a strategy that some internet retailer's use may be considered a short lived virus. Be aware that some online stores will drop the price of items to create a feeding frenzy. After a quantity of people start ordering, the price increases. If you have told friend and family about the deal, they may end up going to the web site and pay full price.

By lowering the price of the item for a short time, it gets people excited and the word spreads! Remember years ago when stores would give away a gallon of milk with any $10 purchase? The milk was the loss leader. The store would take a small loss on the milk in order to lead you into the store. This same strategy is used to get customers to websites. They hope, while you are there, you will shop around and put a few extra things in your cart.

Know Now

How do you know what's on sale before it happens? One method is to sign up for the stores reward or customer loyalty program. Some of these programs are listed below:

Best Buy - Click Rewards zone at the top of their web site.

Staples - https://www.staplesrewardscenter.com

Office Depot - http://www.worklifereward.com/

For a complete list of rewards links visit TheFrugalFactor.com

When signing up for a reward program be sure to provide a good e-mail address. Many stores like OfficeMax will send a weekly e-mail, usually on Thursday that contains a link to the upcoming Sunday sale. Other sites, like Staples.com, list their upcoming sales in a "Sneak Peak" section several days ahead of the actual sale. If you visit their website you should be able to see the advertisement before the Sunday sale.

If you are not enrolled in their rewards program, check the store's web site. Some list their upcoming sales a few days ahead of time.

If you're worried about Spam (unwanted email), sign up for a Yahoo, or hotmail email account. Use the new email account for all of your reward card signups. Also use it for any coupon websites that request an email address when signing up for membership.

The Price Match

If you see an offer on a web site, like Best Buy or Office Depot, print the page! Then go to the store to pick up the product and buy it. Do not worry about the price being wrong. Take the item to your car, then return to the stores customer service department. At the customer service department show them the print out from the web site and request a price match, or price adjustment. Usually there is no problem. A problem occurs only if the website says "on-line only sale".

I did this a few years ago with a DVD recorder I purchased from Best Buy. I shocked the customer service representative a little when she asked who I wanted to price match, and I said Best Buy. I handed her the print out of the web site, showing a price less then half the instore price. She left, verified the price, and credited my credit card for the difference. Before I left she said, "That was a really good deal."

I have discovered some stores will remove items from the shelves when price matches become aggressive. They will store the items in the back until the week passes. So, always pre-purchase the item before requesting a price match. If the price match does not work, simply return the item.

There have been several times when the price I have found on the web site was lower than in the physical store. So, I simply ask them price match their own web site. Web site price matches can also be done if the lower price is from another local store.

One time, at Circuit City, the price match involved a rebate that was only available if the item was purchased online. The customer service representative was kind and explained that one of the rebates was only valid if I placed the order online. Since I was already in the store I went over to the computer department, went online and placed the order for in store pickup. This was actually suggested by the customer service representative. Remember; Always be prepared to return the item if the price match does not work out. (Circuit City went out of business in 2009!)

If you find a price online lower than at the local store request a price match. Recently many stores have made a change and only provide a price match to the <u>after</u> rebate price. If the store does not know there is a rebate at the other store, you can double dip!

If you purchase online, before you call for the price match, be sure that the online retailer that has the lower price is an authorized vendor of the product. Also, include the shipping price in your comparison. If not, the shipping charge may be added to the price before the price match is made. To find out if the online retailer is an authorized dealer, visit the web site of the company that makes the product.

Before you go through the price matching battle prepare yourself. Read the store policy, either at the store, or online. Bring a copy with you, if you are going to a brick and motar store. Some will honor the price match, but tell you that it invalidates their store rebate. I have always found that statement to be false. I always submit and still get the store rebate.

3

In Store Deals

In store deals allow you to use multiple coupons, shop for clearance merchandise, try products before purchasing, easily return undesirable products, and sometimes barter for lower prices.

The Magic of the Buy and Return

If you know an item will be on sale on Sunday, buy it on Thursday or Friday. Why? Hot items at low prices will sell out, moments after the store opens (20 minutes or less). Customers show up before the store opens and wait outside. If you don't want to miss out on the deal, buy the item ahead of time.

Then after the sale starts, return to the store with your receipt. Explain that you bought the item last week and now it's on sale. Ask them to make a price adjustment. Now, be careful, if the item is not just on sale but also includes a rebate, or something free, like a free printer. You will need the store to return the item and re-ring it. You must have a receipt with the correct date for the rebate.

I have done this "Buy and Return" several times, without any problems. One of the best deals was at Best Buy. They had a Toshiba laptop that was going on sale Sunday. I worried that there would not be a large quantity available, and that there would be a line outside the store before it opened. So, I bought the laptop on the Thursday before the sale. When I arrived at the store the laptop was not on display. I spotted the laptop in one of the locked cabinets below the display. I was able to find it because the item number was on the side of the box. Then I found a salesperson, brought him over to the item, and said I would like to buy that laptop. He first asked if I wanted to see the laptop first. I said no, since I knew it was not on display. Then he asked if I wanted it checked out. Best Buy will do a free system check, and attempt to sell you anti virus software and extended warranty. I said, "No, I do not want the box opened in case I needed to return it" I used the excuse that it was a present, and I was not sure if it was what the person wanted.

If the box were opened, there would be a restocking fee. Restocking fees vary by store. The real reason I did not want the laptop opened was that I did not want it at the retail price of $899. I wanted it at the deal price of $599 minus the $100 off coupon for any laptop computer (I printed the coupon from a link I found on the Internet), plus the free printer. Now, if the deal on Sunday did not go through, I would just return the laptop sealed just as I had purchased it.

I returned on Sunday, requested a price adjustment, and the free printer that came with the deal. Best Buy made the price adjustment and gave me the free printer without any problem.

If something does not go right be prepared to return the item. So, keep everything sealed in the original packaging until the price adjustment.

BONUS - after I purchased, INTEL had a special offer providing a Laptop backpack, and a $100 Marriott Reward coupon for buying a laptop with their processor. This made the purchase an even better deal!

Return Policies

Many online retailers have excellent return policies and other do not. Shoe retailer Zappos.com pays shipping costs in both directions, and L.L. Bean will accept merchandise returns a year after they have been purchased. These retailers are focused on building long term relationships with their customers.

One of the key things I look for when buying online is whether or not I can return an item to their local retail store. For example if I find an amazing deal on bath towels at Kohls.com I might hesitate in making the purchase because I cannot actually hold the merchandise. Since Kohl's allows me to return an item to the local store and I found a free shipping code, I made the purchase.

Kohl's offers special discounts to its credit card holders. If you have Kohl's credit card you may receive special discount codes such as free shipping or 30% off. These discounts can only be used when you use your Kohl's card. Kohl's also allows customers to return anything purchased online to their local brick and mortar retail store.

Return policies at warehouse clubs are usually excellent, but often change. At Costco you have 90 days to return most electronics and can return anything else anytime. At Sam club you have six months to return a computer, and can return anything else anytime.

If an item can be returned, and there seems to be a real Frugal deal, buy now and ask questions later. When you arrive at home do a little research on the Internet to see if it was a real frugal deal, and give yourself a little cooling off period. If it's truly a good deal and something that you needed, great. If not return it on your next trip to the store.

Out of Stock

If an item is out of stock, ask the manager when more will arrive in stock. Many managers will tell you, "the truck comes on Tuesday". When you get that kind of information write it down in your coupon binder. When you know deliveries are on Tuesday, then you will want to be at the store early Wednesday. It usually takes a day for the shelves to be restocked. If the item is really important to you, on Tuesday, ask if there are any more in the back room. Some stores can check their computers to see what is supposed to be on the truck. If you use your social engineering skills, you may be able to get them to hold the item for you.

A Taxing Problem

State sales tax can really cause price shock at the register. Remember that you will pay tax on the item's full price before any rebates or many store's instant rebates. In big bold print on the front of one of Sunday's advertisements you see a laptop for only $399. That price is after a $50 instant savings and a $150 rebate. Therefore, the starting price is $599. You will pay state sales tax on the full $599 price. If your state sales tax is 7% you will pay $41.93 in tax. So, the total at the register will be $640.93 - $50 instant savings $590.93. That's far from the $399 price you might have been expecting. So, after your rebate arrives your final price will be $440.93 ($399 + $41.93).

The Warranty

If you have purchased a high cost item, I recommend making a copy of your receipt and taping it to the bottom or back of the product. If the product fails within the warranty you won't be digging through your files looking for a receipt.

Be sure to make a copy. Many receipts are made from thermal paper and will deteriorate over time. After a few months some receipts turn black, or the printing fades away.

It does not matter how great a deal you got when the product stops working. Most experts agree that extended warranties are not worth the money. Usually high tech items (which includes everything that plugs into the wall or takes batteries) will be obsolete before the warranty runs out, or a newer better model is released at a cost lower, than the cost of the extended warranty!

Instead of buying the stores extend warranty, buy a high quality product. How do you know a quality product? Read the "real people" reviews on sites such as Amazon.com. If it's a computer type product go to Newegg.com. By reading the reviews, you will at least eliminate really poor quality products.

Also, if you buy the item with a credit card, the credit card company may double the manufacturers warranty. So, give your credit card company a call and see if they offer this benefit.

Be practical when making your purchases. Electronic items have a short usable life span. But durable products like refrigerators, dishwashers, and clothes washers may last over ten years. Our current clothes washer is over twenty years old and has never needed a repair.

On these durable products it's wise to get the features you want since you will be living with the product for many years.

If one of your appliances breaks down after the warranty period use the Internet to look for a solution. There are many "do it yourself" repair sites which will provide parts and instructions for most appliances.

A few years back our refrigerator icemaker stopped working. A quick search with the make and model number and I found the part and installation instructions. The fix required only removing two screws and cost less than $70.

Top Review sites:
ConsumerSearch.com
Epinions.com
Amazon.com
Newegg.com

Code 995

Social Engineering

When calling to request a price match, rebate, or clarify a coupons use, remember that the CSR (Customer Service Representative) on the phone has had to deal with rude and difficult people all day long. Having your facts ready, and all the data in front of you, makes their job easier. When talking to the CSR say something like "I hope you can help me out. I bought (name of product) and the price at (name of cheaper store) is lower. Is there any chance you can price match the item, or possibly cancel my order?"

When you ask someone to help you, instead of being demanding, it takes the pressure off both parties. Remember to always be prepared to return the item if the deal does not work. Also, always know the return policy of the stores you deal with. At many stores technology items must be returned within 14 days. Open technology items may also have a restocking fee.

I had a situation were I purchased a cordless phone with multiple handsets from an online office supply store. On their web site was a coupon code to reduce the price of the item. When I got to the checkout I entered the code, but it did not take. Knowing the store well and having purchased from them many times in the past, I knew it would not be a problem.

I printed the website page showing the coupon code and the product page, after the order was complete I called their 800 number. The CSR on the phone made the price adjustment for me. No problem.

But about a week later in another office supply store, I saw a flyer with the same phone on sale for $30 less. Being that the stores were only about 3 miles apart, I took the flyer and went to the store I purchase the phone from.

I asked to talk to the manager. After explaining the situation the manager called the Internet division of the company and explained what had happened. The manager argued on my behalf with the Internet division Customer Service Representative (CSR). They would not do a price match because a price match had already been done.

Well, in reality a price match had not been done. Since the coupon code did not work, the original CSR put the price adjustment in as a price match, and even though it was to their own web site they would only do one price match, or price adjustment. They would only price match once even if it was their error.

The manager handed me the phone and I continued to calmly explain that the price match was due to an error on their website because it would not take their own coupon code. The Internet CSR would not budge. I made a comment on the phone that the only power I had as a consumer was to no longer shop at the store. I then handed the phone back to the manager. She hung up the phone and I thank her for trying. To my surprise, she then asked me for my credit card, and verified with me the price I paid. The store manager then credited to my card the difference in price. While I got poor customer service from the Internet CSR, the store manager went above and beyond my expectations by doing the price match.

Always know the policy of the store's price match and return policy.

Remember the greatest power you have, as a consumer is to shop someplace else, and to tell your friends and neighbors about your experiences.

Not So Secret Codes

Some stores have secret-pricing codes they use to indicate an item's status, last stock, seasonal or final markdown. At my local Sam's Club, an item ending in $0.01 is the last of that item that will be stocked. This often happens with seasonal items. At Costco anytime you see a Costco in-store price that ends in $0.97 you know that the item has been discounted from its original selling price.

Sam's club uses a **C** to identify discontinued items and Costco uses a "*". Now these codes may change at any time. If you keep a close eye on a few products it's easy to discover new codes. Usually if you ask a manager or knowledgeable employee, they will confirm the codes.

Gift Cards

Why do stores offer gift cards? A high percentage of gift cards are never used. Given as birthday or Christmas presents, many gift cards are never redeemed. Others are never redeemed for the full value. Many will use a gift card only one time, whether or not they used the entire value of the card. Some cards are carried around for years in wallets and purses.

Experts estimate that value of unused gift cards at over 8 billion dollars. Some retailers have gained a profit of over 40 million dollars in gift cards that are unlikely to be used.

A new twist in gift cards is a monthly fee. After six months or a year, some cards start charging a monthly fee. After a few months your gift card may be worthless! Always check the terms of the gift card before you buy.

Want to give a gift card as a present, Don't! Instead, call a local bank or credit union and see if they offer Visa gift cards. My bank offers Visa gift cards in any amount up to $500. They charge a one-dollar fee, regardless of the amount of the card. The benefit: the Visa gift card can be used at any store that takes Visa.

Remember there are few regulations covering gift cards. The risk of unauthorized purchases rest with the cardholder. So, if the card is lost or the issuer goes out of business your out of luck!

Check the fine print on all gift cards. Check for monthly fees, expiration dates on the card, or on the issuers web site. Be aware that card issuer's reserve the right to change their terms at any time. If it's a gift card, they do not have to give you notice. Even if they wanted to, they don't have your address.

4

Grocery Stores

Knowing your local store policies, using multiple coupons and price matching are all keys to successful grocery and superstore shopping.

Coupons

Grocery coupons first appeared in the late 1800's. Coca-Cola distributed hand written tickets for a free glass of soda and C.W. Post distributed one-cent coupons for their Grape Nuts cereal. In the 1930's coupons made a big impact as households attempted to save money in any way they could during the Great Depression.

Today there are literally thousands of grocery coupons available. A common source of grocery store coupons is the Sunday newspapers, Smart Source and RedPlum inserts. To become a frugal shopper you need to start your coupon collection. Start collecting as many coupons as you can from the following sources:

> Sunday Newspapers
> Online Web Sites
> Manufacturer's Web sites
> Store Tearpads

If you find several good coupons in the Sunday paper, it might be profitable to purchase extra papers. Also, when you find a tearpad on a shelf always take a few extra. you never know when you will need them, especially when the expiration dates are far into the future.

Price Knowledge

You must know product prices in order to find a frugal deal. For example if a gallon of milk is usually $3.99, and on sale for $1.99 you have found a good deal. It can become a real Frugal deal if you have a coupon to further reduce the price.

Create your own list of items you commonly purchase and write down the standard price that you expect to pay. Constantly update your list. This may sound like a lot of work, but your only going to keep track of items you constantly purchase. By doing this you will know when a price is good enough to start stockpiling.

Smart Couponing

Don't use a coupon on a name brand product that is still more expensive than the store brand. For example, if the store brand of paper napkins are less expensive, even after you apply the coupon to the national brand, buy the store brand. You will find many coupons in the newspaper every week for highly overprice items. Even after using the coupon many of these products are still not Frugal deals.

Note: sometimes a coupon may work on the trial sizes!

Local Deals

Find out the policy of your local store. They may have certain days that they will double or triple the value of a coupon. They may offer you free items if you find an expired item still on their shelves. Expired items are often found in the meat and bread sections of the stores.

Almost all grocery stores will give you the item free, if it rings up on the register with the wrong price. So, keep an eye on the register and know the price of what you are buying. It almost turns into a game.

Competition

Find out which stores in your area will honor competitor coupons. My local grocery store will take CVS Extrabucks and Walgreen's coupons. Home Depot and Lowes honor each other coupons and so do most of the competing office supply stores. Some stores even accept expired coupons.

Putting it on the conveyor.

Help the cashiers by placing the UPC symbols facing them or down so that they can be scanned easily. If you have a coupon that requires the cashier to write in the price of the item, place that item on the conveyor last. This way the cashier does not need to scroll through the entire list of items to find the price. Also, place those coupons on the top of the stack.

When you have a large stack of coupons alternate the coupon types so the cashier does not miss any. Place newspaper coupons between the Internet coupons. If you have many duplicate or Internet coupons, wrinkle them so they do not stick together.

Store Policy

Know the store's coupon and return policy. If it's on their web site, print and keep a copy with your coupons. Many times the cashier or even manager does not know his or her own corporate policy.

Sometimes there is an overage. That means the coupon exceeds the price of the item. Often, the overage is simply applied to the total value of your purchase. Sometimes a cashier will notice that the item costs $2.84 and your coupon is for $4 and not allow you to use it. When this happens calmly request that they adjust the coupon down the value of the item or simply don't buy the item. Often, I won't buy the item because I know the next time I will get a cashier that will simply take the total amount of the coupon from the total purchase.

Read the Coupons

A coupon may state one per purchase, which really means one per item. You are purchasing each item right! Sometimes a cashier will say they must ring each item separately if I want to use all those coupons. They usually expect me to back down. I don't mind watching them work more while I wait. If they simply refuse, ask for the manager. If the manager refuses to take your coupons, calmly ask their name and the stores corporate identification number. Then let them know that you will be happy to call or write the corporate office to get clarification of the policy. Always be polite. They are just doing their job as they have been trained.

I have made phone calls from every major drug store, supermarket and office supply store in my area. This call is always to get clarification on a discount, rebate, or the store's coupon policy. The managers and cashiers are usually shocked to see me pull out my cell phone right in front of them and make the call.

If I get the answer I wanted, I then tell the customer service representative on the phone that I am in the store and ask if they wouldn't mind explaining it to a store employee. Then I hand my phone to the store manager or cashier.

I always tell them that I want consistency from store to store and that I am just trying to feed my family. Sometimes I get different reactions to coupons from the same retail chain and that's just not right.

If the coupon states, "One per order," or, "One per transaction," it means you can only use one coupon per register transaction. Usually the register will not allow the cashier to override the coupon. This is when you must ask the cashier to ring each one up individually.

If a coupon states "One per customer," you are only supposed to be able to use one per visit to the store. When this happens, I simply make the purchase, bring the item out to the car and return for the next purchase. Now, if you have your entire family with you, put them to work. When it states one per customer, and a cashier has a problem with me buying more than one item, I simply hand a few dollars to each one of my children and have them purchase the items for me. I did this at an office supply store when a new manager enforced the one per customer rule. After I purchased my one item I picked my children up from school and we all went back and purchased the quantity I originally wanted. Now, this will not work if you need to use a customer loyalty card the buy the item. Unless of course you have more than one loyalty card!

Buy one Get one Free (BOGO) are wonderful coupons. Combine them with cents off coupons and I can often get two items for free instead of just one.

Remember that the store gets fully reimbursed for the coupon from the manufacturer, plus an additional fee usually about eight cents per coupon. There have been times I needed to remind the manager that the store does not loose money by taking my coupons. They actually gain eight cents and retain a customer.

Pharmacy Deals

Most drug stores offer a $25 gift card if you transfer your prescription. When my children needed some type of medication I would always get a pharmacy gift card. The next time a prescription was needed I would switch pharmacies and get another gift card.

If you need prescription medications daily have your doctor write a three-month prescription. This way you will only have to pay the co-payment once every three months.

Also, shop around for the best price. Check out Sam's Club, Wal-Mart, Target, and Costco. You do not need a membership to buy prescription drugs from one of the warehouse clubs.

Note: There are often valuable coupons in the information booklets posted near the pharmacy.

Cashier Profiling

As you start using more and more coupons, it's important to select the cashier who is working for you, not the store. Newly trained employees may be scared about doing something wrong when taking a coupon. You want to spot the experienced cashier that is easy going and is working for the hourly wage. You simply want someone on your side.

It's important to talk to the cashier and let them know you have coupons. I often tell them "I'm trouble", "I have lots of coupons", or something like, " the coupon man is here". They usually just smile, laugh or say "That's OK". Inside, I am sure they're saying "This guy is crazy". I never show them the coupons until after all the groceries have been scanned. Sometimes the number of coupons that I have surprises them.

Once, at a local superstore, I was checking out at a register by a cashier I use often. I watched the cashier ring up each item, and made small talk with her (social engineering is important). I was holding my 40+ coupons in my hand. Then a man came out of an office and headed directly to me and asked if he could see my coupons. I said sure, and gave him my stack. He sorted them out and looked carefully at each one. Then he stacked them up and gave them back. I asked if there was anything wrong. He simply said "no", and went back through the door. All I can figure was that they must have seen my large stack of coupons from the security cameras. I now keep all the coupons in my pocket or binder until I see the register total.

I seldom have any problems with the cashiers taking a coupon. Over time I have gotten to know which cashiers at each store are easy going and not overly critical. Basically, if the coupon will scan, they will take it.

But every once in a while you run across a cashier who will read the fine print on the coupons. I know a few cashiers that have scanned a coupon and the register accepts it, then they look at the coupon again and see that it states a purchase of a 20-ounce product, and I purchased 24-ounce product. My family affectionately calls these cashiers "Coupon Nazi's", Sometimes the store does not even carry he right size for the coupon. Even though the register accepted the coupon, they won't allow me to use it. This happened several times when Pepsi switched from twelve packs to eight packs.

Of course the "Coupon Nazi" is just doing their job. Sometimes it's just the attitude and body language the cashier displays, that is very upsetting. I have had cashiers huff and puff with attitude and complain as they manually type the code of each coupon into the computer, because their hand scanner was not working properly. It was as if they expected my to say, "Never mind. Don't use the coupons." As a customer, it was not my fault the equipment was faulty. I just patiently watched, and after the ordeal made a note not to get in that cashier's line ever again.

Sometimes, before we get to the register I will make a quick comment to my wife "register 9 is a Coupon Nazi, but register 7 is a friend of mine". They are not actually friends of mine, I just know that in the past they have accepted my stack of coupons without a problem and had a good attitude.

There have been times that I have needed to warn a cashier that they scanned a coupon twice, so that they could remove the credit. Why would I do something crazy like this? To avoid a negative balance. At times I have bought several items and the store owed me money! Stores usually won't open the cash register and hand you the overage.

Once, after Halloween, Target marked down bags of M&M's to 86 cents. At the same time on the Target website was a coupon for $1 off any bag of M&M's. You guessed right, I bought almost all of the M&M's (over 50 large bags) and paid less than $2 for all of them.

If you ever have a coupon dispute remember your social engineering skills. Most of the time its best to just stay silent, which is sometimes hard to do. If the decision does not go your way let the manager know that you have a voice and will be talking to friends about your experience in the store, be sure to do it in a nice way.

When things do go your way be sure to spread the word. Let people know that you're happy with a certain store or service. There are very few businesses that I can recommend without hesitation. For me over the past 20 year there are only two that have never failed to provide excellent service. One is my veterinarian and the other my car mechanic. I am sure that over the years, through my referrals, I have brought them thousands of dollars of business.

When you leave the store take a minute to review your receipt and decide how you did. Do not believe the, "You Saved", comment at the bottom of most store receipts. Take a good look at each item and the coupons used. Some store receipts are more difficult to read than others. Be sure that each coupon was scanned and that you did not get charged double on any item.

Be honest with yourself. Did you do good, bad, or excellent! What items should you have left behind, and which did you get for free, or even better, have an overage? When you selected the register line to stand in, did you pick a good cashier? Did the cashier have any problems with your coupons?

By doing this quick critique you will increase your frugal skills, which will lead to more successful shopping trips.

Family Competition

It's easier to become frugal when you involve the entire family. If you have children, it's also a great learning experience. Let them use a calculator and have them figure out which product is a better deal. Have them calculate the cost per ounce or quantity. For example brand A of laundry detergent is $12 for 100 ounces and brand B is $4.50 for 32 ounces. Therefore, brand A is 12 cents per ounce and brand B is 14 cents per ounce. Brand A is a better deal.

My wife and I also compare who can get the best deal. When a store limits items one per customer or loyalty card, we will both go shopping. Using similar coupons we will try to out do each other by getting the most product with the least amount of money out of pocket.

Stockpiling

Ever run out of toilet paper and wish you had a roll in a glass case that said, "Break only in emergency." OK, a glass case may not be a good idea, but you get my meaning. That's why careful planning and stockpiling will not only save you money, but it can also create less stress in your life.

Stockpiling cleaning supplies and paper products is a no brainer. But when stockpiling food you need to watch the expiration dates. For example, you don't want to stockpile more cereal than your family can eat. Keep on eye on your stockpile expiration dates. If your family can't consume it all in time, donate it to a homeless shelter, or to family and friends.

Some items to stockpile include:

Shampoo
Razors,
Canned Goods, Cereal
Laundry Detergent
Paper Products

Grocery Coupon Web Sites

There are many different grocery coupon web sites. Here are a few good ones to check out. For a complete list with direct links visit the TheFrugalFactor.com website.

Coupons.com
CouponMom.com
SmartSource.com
Wow-coupons.com

Bricks coupons

Coupons that are commonly called "bricks coupons" are coupons from couponsinc.com that have a limit to the number of times they can be printed. A code is placed on your computer so it will only print a certain number of times. Usually after printing the coupon the first time you can hit the back button on your browser three time to get it to print a second time.

Of course, if you have another computer, you can use it to print another coupon.

Loyalty Cards

Grocery stores and drug stores have loyalty cards. These cards provide in-store discounts and help the store track your purchases. The store can easily use these cards to build a personal profile of you, and your buying habits. This enables them to keep the right items in stock at local stores, and helps them target market special offers and coupons to the individual customers.

Some stores offer discounts when you use their loyalty cards. CVS has an excellent program for their customers, and the store. Each week a customer can get a discount or even receive an item free after "extra bucks." Extrabucks is a reward printed at the bottom of your receipt. For example CVS advertises "Aspirin $3.99 Free after Extra bucks". You purchase the aspirin and pay $3.99. At the bottom of your receipt you have a coupon for $3.99. The Extrabucks coupons can be used on your next purchase.

CVS has successfully captured your money, and at the same time almost ensures that you will return to the store to spend the Extrabucks. Excellent marketing on CVS's part! Walgreen's has a similar system called Register Rewards. About once a month CVS will provide an item "Free after Extra Bucks". Sometimes you can even find a coupon in the newspaper or online for the same product. That makes the item less than free. Yes, you make money. This is commonly called an overage. Now, the store will not open its register and hand you cash. You will need to purchase some other product and the overage amount will be taken from that product's cost.

Tracking

Most stores use the loyalty cards to track your purchases. This can be a good thing and a bad thing. The good is that it allows the store to know what merchandise to stock at each of its stores and the frequency of their customer's purchases.

The loyalty card tracks who buys what. The information can be used to strategically raise profits by raising prices. You see, the top 20% of the customers give the store 80% of the profits. The cards allow the store to keep the top twenty percent happy by always having the products those customers want in stock, at the stores they shop at.

The card data can also tell a store if you are willing to pay $4.99 for an item that is usually $3.99. By using this data the store can estimate your price/pain threshold. If a high percentage of the top customers will still buy the item at $4.99, will they still buy the item at $5.99? If the answer is yes, you will see the price increase until the store is making what it calculates as the greatest profit on the item.

So, remember each time you use your loyalty card you are voting for the prices that you are paying! If you're frugal you can use the loyalty card to your advantage.

Shrinkage

The forever shrinking packages! While you can biggie size it at your local fast food restaurant, the product sizes in the supermarkets are shrinking fast.

What the industry calls, "downsizing" is what manufactures have done to offset the increasing cost of ingredients and to increase profits. Since the price remains the same, and the outside package is the same size, some consumers have not noticed the amount of product in the package is less.

My favorite ice cream once came in a two-quart package. Now it's only 1.5 quarts. Here is a list of a few items that have been downsized:

Ice Cream
Cereal Boxes
Bags of chips
Orange Juice
Soap
Cookies
Soda from 12 packs to 8 packs

Always compare packages to see which one will give you the best value when using your coupons.

The Pass Back

There are times when a store provides a gift card attached to certain products. When it happens it usually limited to one per customer. The way around this is to have many customers with you. I have a family of five. So, when Target put 12 packs of Pepsi products on sale, four twelve packs for $10 they also provided a $5 gift card. You don't need to be a math genius to figure out that $5 for 4 - 12 packs, is a good deal. OK, I will do the math for you. That's $1.25 per 12 pack, or 10.4 cents per can. So, we went SHOPPING!

The entire family went to Target. Each one of us got a shopping cart and placed four - 12 packs of Pepsi products in each cart. We then followed each other to register. When I paid for the first order I received my $5 gift card at the register. I handed the card back to my wife, who used it to pay for part of her order. She received a $5 gift card and passed it back to my daughter and so on...

We ended up with twenty-five, twelve packs of soda and a $5 gift card at the end. We then let the children use the remaining $5 gift card at Target's Dollar Spot. The Dollar Spot is an area in the front of the store with items for; ...you guessed it... one dollar (or more). My wife gets full credit for this "Pass Back" idea. I was excited about the discount and just thought we would use the gift cards when there was another good deal at Target.

Understanding UPC Codes

Being able to read UPC codes can help your coupon strategy. GS1 is the organization that provides the standard bar codes for the United States. The UPC code of a coupon is like a hidden language. You can decode the numbers to unlock the hidden language

So find a coupon and let's decipher the code.

1. First ignore the small 5 or 9 at the beginning of the coupon. A 5 tells the point of sale system that it's scanning a coupon. A 9 is a coupon distributed in the store. Coupons that begin with 9 will not be doubled by the grocery store.

2. Take a look at the first 5 digits under the bar code. These numbers are the manufacturer's code. The manufacturer's code will be the same on all of the manufacturer coupons.

3. The next three digits are the family code. The family code identifies products, or groups of products the coupon is valid on. This code validates that a consumer has purchased the correct product corresponding to the terms

of the coupon. The manufacturer must fit all of the different sizes, colors, forms, fragrances and more into these three digits.

If there is one zero at the end, the coupon will work for more than one variety or size of the product. If there are two zero's at the end the coupon will work for more than one type or brand of product.

Often, I can use the coupon on a lower cost product (like trial size). This creates an overage, making the product less than free, and a real Frugal deal.

A family code of 000 usually indicates that the coupon will work on any product with the same manufacturer code. Family codes between 990 and 999 are reserved, therefore no product verification will take place when the coupon is scanned. So, basically it will work on any product from the designated manufacturer! Family codes are created by the manufacturer and can change at any time.

For example the family code of 992 on a coupon will always be accepted, even if you did not purchase the item, or always make the register beep. Whether the coupon beeps or not, depends on how the store has its registers programmed. When the register beeps it requires a manual override from the cashier.

4. The next two digits represent the coupon value. The value of the codes are listed on the next page.

5. The last digit of the barcode is the computer check digit, which makes sure the barcode is correctly composed for the point of sale system to read.

Code	Value	Code	Value
01	Free Merchandise	51	Buy 2+ get $2.00 off
02	Buy 4 Get 1 Free	52	Buy 3+ get $0.55 off
03	$1.10	53	Buy 2+ get $0.10 off
04	$1.35	54	Buy 2+ get $0.15 off
05	$1.40	55	$0.55
06	$1.60	56	Buy 2+ get $0.20 off
07	Buy 3+ get $1.50 off	57	Buy 2 get $0.25 off
08	Buy 2+ get $3.00 off	58	Buy 2 Get $0.30 off
09	Buy 3+ get $2.00 off	59	$0.59
10	$0.10	60	$0.60
11	$1.85	61	$10.00
12	$0.12	62	$9.50
13	Buy 4+ get $1.00 off	63	$9.00
14	Buy 1 get one Free	64	$0.50
15	$0.15	65	$0.65
16	Buy 2 get 1 Free	66	$8.00
17	Reserved for future use	67	$7.50
18	$2.60	68	$7.00
19	Buy 3 get one Free	69	$0.69
20	$0.20	70	$0.70
21	Buy 2+ get $0.35 off	71	$6.50
22	Buy 2+ get $0.40 off	72	$6.00
23	Buy 2+ get $0.45 off	73	$5.50
24	Buy 2+ get $0.50 off	74	$5.00
25	$0.25	75	$0.75
26	$2.85	76	$1.00
27	Reserved for future use	77	$1.25
28	Buy 2 get $0.55 off	78	$1.50
29	$0.29	79	$0.79
30	$0.30	80	$0.80
31	Buy 2+ get $0.60 off	81	$1.75
32	Buy 2+ get $0.75 off	82	$2.00
33	Buy 2 get $1.00 off	83	$2.25
34	Buy 2+ get $1.25 off	84	$2.50
35	$0.35	85	$0.85
36	Buy 2+ get $1.50 off	86	$2.75
37	Buy 3+ get $0.25 off	87	$3.00

38	Buy 3+ get $0.30 off	88	$3.25
39	$0.39	89	$0.89
40	$0.40	90	$0.90
41	Buy 3+ get $0.50 off	91	$3.50
42	Buy 3+ get $1.00 off	92	$3.75
43	Buy 2+ get $1.10 off	93	$4.00
44	Buy 2+ get $1.35 off	94	Reserved for future use
45	$0.45	95	$0.95
46	Buy 2+ get $1.60 off	96	$4.50
47	Buy 2+ get $1.75 off	97	Reserved for future use
48	Buy 2+ get $1.85 off	98	Buy 2+ get $0.65 off
49	$0.49	99	$0.99
50	$0.50	00	Checker intervention

Code 4321

RainChecks

When you find free or almost free items, stock up! Even buy more than you can use, and donate it to a school, homeless shelter or other charity.

Often products are given away free with a coupon, so that you will buy the refill. Razor blades and air fresheners are good examples. The razor blades usually contain one cartridge. If I can, I will buy lots of these items for FREE, that way I never need to buy the refills. It's been a very long time since I purchased a pack of razor blades!

Always ask for a rain check if a sale item is out of stock. Rain checks can give you additional flexibility. Some RainChecks will offer, "Choose a substitute and get the same percentage off on a similar, regular priced item."

Often when an item is out of stock the store will place a tear pad of RainChecks on the shelf. Simply fill out the form indicating the quantity you want and take it to the register.

So, if you find an item you really want, find a similar item that is out of stock. Bring the out of stock items rain check to the customer service department and request the rain check. While you are there ask if you can substitute an in stock item for the same percentage off. If you use your social engineering skills you will probably get a discount on the item you really wanted all along.

Note: Many stores do not offer RainChecks or substitutes for electronic items.

Organizing Coupons

As you start building your coupon collection it can get out of hand quickly. Now, is a good time to start organizing. There is no right or wrong way to organize your coupons. Different systems work for different people. Grocery coupons can be placed in envelopes, accordion files, or even a photo album. I think sorting alphabetically is crazy! Sorting by product type works. Even better, sort by store aisle.

Your local store probably has a printed layout of its aisle's readily available near customer service counter. Pick up one or more of these printouts and use it to organize your coupons. In the past I discarded coupons for products I thought I would never buy, only to later find another coupon, making the item completely free. So, even if you think, "I would never buy that," keep those coupons in a special spot.

As far as organizing the coupons, I like a three-ring zipper binder with clear inserts. Inserts that are used for photo albums and trading cards work well.

See a photo of my binder at TheFrugalFactor.com website.

5

Credit Cards

Credit cards can be both a blessing and a curse. If used correctly, credit cards can be convenient and profitable. The following pages will show you how to make extra money when you use credit cards wisely.

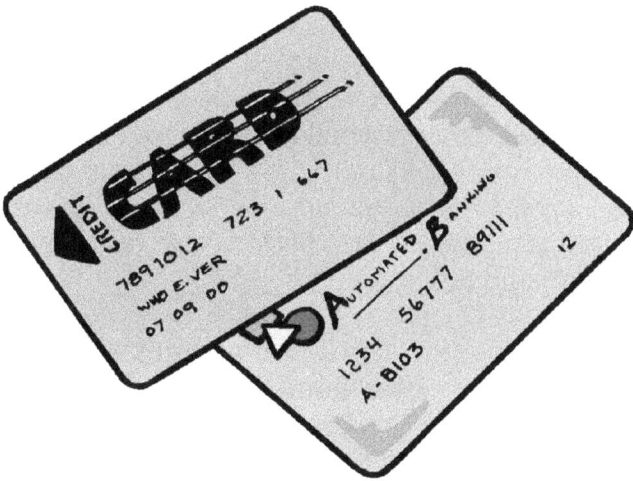

Credit Card Deals

To be truly Frugal, if you have a balance each month on your credit card, you need to pay it off as soon as possible. You can actually benefit and make money with your credit cards. This will only work if you have good credit and you <u>do not</u> carry a balance on **any** credit cards.

Keys to selecting a credit card. You should always have more than one credit card. I can't believe I just said that! I went for years with only one. If you have the willpower you can profit from a few extra credit cards.

Credit cards have their benefits. First, not all cards are universally excepted. You can't make a purchase at Sam's Club with a Visa card, but they accept Discover and MasterCard. So, having different brands of cards can be an advantage. But the real benefit comes in the form of sign up bonuses and rewards.

Chase and Citibank have several cards that offer both a sign up bonus and cash back rewards. I currently have one card that provides 5% cash back for gas, grocery and drugs stores. Another card provides 3% cash back on gas, restaurants, home improvement, and office supply stores.

Every month I log into my Chase account and look at my rewards. When I have over 5,000 points I click a few buttons and have them apply a $50 credit to my account. I can also select a store gift card or have them send me a check. It's simply easier to have them apply the credit directly to the card's next billing cycle.

There are many different types of rewards. You need to find the one that provides you with the most benefit for your lifestyle. From me it's cash. Others might choose hotels or airline rewards.

This all started a few years ago when American Express sent me a pre-approved offer for their Gold Card. I usually toss these in the garbage, but this one came in a large envelope, which got me to open it. Good marketing on American Express's part. When I opened the envelope and read all of the fine print I decided to accept their offer. If I accepted the American Express Gold card, the yearly fee would be waived for the first year and I would receive 25,000 points in their rewards program if I spent $500 within the first three months.

I looked at their reward website and discovered I could redeem the 25,000 points for a $250 Home Depot Gift card. Which is exactly what I did. I used the card and carefully kept track of my spending. When I reached the $500 level I stopped using the card. On the next bill I saw the 25,000 points credited to my account. After I received my reward I put the card away and did not use it. You need to have the willpower to put the card away, not use it, or cut it up if necessary. Most people keep spending. This is how the credit card companies can continue to make these offers. Remember if the card has an annual fee cancel it before the twelve-month anniversary.

Now, my wife also had the same offer. So, between the two of us we had $500 to spend at Home Depot. We used the gift cards to paint the inside of our house. Now every time I look around I can smile, remembering the deal.

I have done similar things with over a dozen credit cards over the years. One sent me a check for $200 after my first purchase. Another required a single purchase over $299 before I would receive a $100 statement credit. For that one I simply went to Wal-Mart and bought a Wal-Mart gift card for $305, when my first statement appeared I only had to pay $205, for the gift card. An instant $100 profit. My other favorites are hotel cards that provide a free night or two for signing up.

These are just a few of the bonus offers I have completed:

Chase Freedom	$200 Check
BOA Iowa Alumni	$250 Check
Sony	$100 Statement Credit
Chase Starwood	Free Hotel Nights
Citi Professional	$135 in Gift Cards
Laquita	Free Hotel Nights
Discover Card	$125 in Gift Cards
CitiForward Card	$100 in Gift Cards

Using these and other offers my family and I have received over $3,000 in benefits over the past three years.

The highest cash back card without any limits is the Schwab Visa card. The Schwab Visa automatically deposits 2% cash back into your brokerage account each month. For links to current credit card deals visit TheFrugalFactor.com.

Frugal Stacking

At times you can double up, or even triple up on a deal. When I needed new tires on my car I began researching tire prices. Using the internet, I discovered that a Discount Tire store would be having a grand opening in about two weeks. During their two-day grand opening celebration they offered $100 off a set of 4 tires. In addition, Michelin offered a $70 rebate off 4 tires. Plus, if I opened a Discount Tire credit card, I would receive a $50 rebate.

I called several competing stores to get prices on the same or similar tires rated at an 80,000 mile tread wear life. One competitor had tires at about $5 less per tire. Then I called Discount Tire. In the past I had always been successful at priced matching tires. This time they would not price match.

When I pushed the salesman a little, telling him how good a customer I was, he told me about the grand opening deal. I explained that I already knew about the deal and was hoping I could also get the price match. This time I did not get the price match, but did confirm with the salesman that I could get all three-price reductions at the same time. I still got an excellent deal, I bought four 80,000 mile Michelin tires (tire size 185/65R14), with lifetime balance and rotation, for the out of pocket cost of $125.

Cost of 4 tires with tax.	$345
Grand Opening Discount	-$100
Discount Tire Credit Card Discount	-$50
Michelin Tire Rebate	-$70
Final Price	**$125**

Things to watch out for:

Annual fees - some have no fees. Other have the fees but they are waived for the first year. Some have large fees. Often, airline rewards cards have an annual fee. The highest yearly card fee I could find was $2,500 for the American Express Centurion Card.

Cash Advances - Be careful cash advance fees and interest rates may be fixed or variable. I have never used my credit card for a cash advance. I simply can't afford to do it.

Balance transfer - If you carry a balance, which is a really bad thing to do, you may be able to transfer the balance from a high interest rate to a lower interest rate. Some cards will even provide 0%, or a very low interest rate, for a limited period of time for new applicants. If you are carrying a balance, pay it off as quickly as possible. Remember, you can make a payment on your card at any time. You do not need to wait until you get your bill.

Now, the strategy is to use the right card at the right store. If I am shopping at Home Depot or Lowes I use the card that provides 3% cash back on home improvement purchases, plus I will use a coupon. Often one of these stores will have a $10 off $50 coupon, or I can usually find a 10% coupon in the change of address kit available free from your local post office.

Benefits

All credit cards are not the same. Some cards have additional features that you can use to your advantage. Features to look for:

- ◆ Zero Liability
- ◆ Car Rental insurance
- ◆ Purchase Protection
- ◆ Extended warranties
- ◆ Virtual Card Numbers
- ◆ Billing disputes
- ◆ Cash Back

Zero Liability - Many credit card issuers provide a zero liability once you report an unauthorized purchase. The coverage of this policy varies from each brand of card. Remember even without the card's zero liability, according to the fair credit billing act you only have to pay a $50 maximum (if reported within 60 days) no matter how much was illegally charged to your card.

Car Rental Insurance – Instead of paying the car rental insurance use you credit card. Most cards will cover the insurance, but this varies from card to card and some states are not covered. Be sure to check that the state you are renting the car from is covered with your card issuer.

Purchase protection - Many cards will protect your new purchase against theft for the first 90 days of ownership.

Extended warranties - Some credit cards will extend the manufacturer warranty up to a year, add an additional year, or double the manufacturer's warranty.

Virtual Card Number - Bank of America, Citibank, and Discover all offer virtual credit card numbers. These virtual numbers link back to your account but can only be used as you specify. For example, When you log into your account on the credit card issuer's web site, you can create a virtual number for each transaction, or set up a number for recurring purchases of a specific amount. The CitiForward credit card allows you to set an amount and expiration date for each virtual card number you create.

If you purchase some type of subscription service that automatically charges you each month or each year, always use a virtual credit card number or a prepaid Visa card.

Since the number is only good once, or how you specify at creation, you can't be charged again without the merchant contacting you for a new billing method. You can then decide if you want to cancel the service.

If your card issuer does not offer virtual card numbers use a prepaid Visa card. Many banks and drugstores offer these cards for a low fee.

If you have a $100 prepaid Visa card a merchant can not charge more than $100 against the card. By the time the subscription is due you may have used up the entire card.

Debit cards withdraw money directly form your bank accounts. The laws for debit cards are not as strict as for credit cards which makes credit cards much safer to use. By using a credit card you put barrier between you and the merchant. If you have a dispute, the credit card company will handle it on your behalf. While in dispute, you still have your money. If you had used a debit card, the money would have disappeared from your bank account, so you would have very little leverage to get a resolution with the merchant.

Free Credit Report

In 2003 the passage of the Fair and Accurate Credit Transaction Act entitled all Americans to one free credit report from each of the three major credit reporting agencies: Equifax, Experian and TransUnion, every 12 months. To request your free credit report visit AnnualCreditReport.com or call 877-322-8228

You can get a copy of your credit report for free every year. Since there are three major credit reporting agencies the smart thing to do is request a report from one of them every four months. By doing this you can quickly find and report any discrepancy or errors.

Credit Score

What effect will taking out multiple credit cards have on your credit score? That all depends on your score. A credit or FICO score is a number ranging from 300 to 850. Most people will have a score between 600 and 800. A score above 720 will get you the most favorable interest rates on a loan or mortgage.

There are five main factors that effect your credit score.

1. Paying your bills on time accounts for 35% of your credit score. Having a long history of making payments on time, with no missed payments has the greatest effect on your FICO score.

2. The amount of money you owe and your available credit accounts for 30% of your credit score. If you are maxing out your credit cards, using all of your available credit, your credit score will drop. Someone close to their credit limit is considered to be at a higher risk for future late payments. FICO scores reward people who are using a smaller percentage of their available credit. This is why it is a good idea to keep credit card accounts open.

   No balance is great, but a dormant credit account will not help your score. So rotate and use all of your credit cards. Charging a few dollars on each card will keep the account active and help your FICO score. Be sure to pay the cards off in full each month.

3. Credit history length accounts for 15% of your credit score. The longer you have had credit the better. Your oldest account and the average age of all your accounts are

considered. Especially if it's with the same credit issuers. So, if you have had the same credit card for ten years or more, don't cancel the account.

4. Mix of credit accounts for 10% of your credit score. People with the best credit scores will have many different types of accounts such as mortgages, car loans and credit cards.

5. New Credit Applications account for 10% of your credit score. Opening several new accounts in a short period of time can lower your credit score. Multiple credit report inquiries can indicate a greater risk. But this does not include requests made by you, your employer, or lenders that send unsolicited pre-approved offers. Also to compensate for interest rate shopping, the score counts multiple inquires in a 14 day period as a single inquiry. So, if you want to apply for several credit cards, that have sign up bonuses, and other rewards, do them all within the same week.

6

Printer Deals

Selecting the right printer and using both color and laser printers can be the frugal thing to do. Use the tips that follow to lower your printer expenses.

Printer Secrets

What printer companies don't want you to know! As many of us know the cost of an inkjet printer is nothing compared to the price of the ink. Some inkjet printer cartridges are over $30 for color and $20 for black. Some of these printers originally sold for less than $50, (after rebate of course) so couldn't you just buy a new printer instead of buying new ink cartridges? Hey the price is almost the same. The answer is NO. The reason is that the printer companies only provide what is called a starter cartridge. Starter cartridges may have less than half the life of a full printer cartridge. The printer companies make their money on selling you new ink and toner cartridges. That's one of the reasons printers are almost given away when you buy a new computer.

Today many printer companies have installed a chip on their ink and toner cartridges. This chip counts the number of pages. Even if the cartridge is not empty the printer will stop after a set number of pages. This chip is often found on inkjet and color laser printers. Some of these chips can be replaced or reset. You can find these chips and reset devices on Bay!

Buy generic ink cartridges! Why? Simple they are much cheaper. My Canon printer takes 4 separate cartridges. Each one sells for $15. That's a total of $60 for one change of ink. Instead of buying the Canon brand ink, I buy generic. The cost of generic ink for the printer is just 99 cents each, or $3.96 for a change of ink.

Now some may say the generic ink is not as good. I have never had a problem. Once in a while I do get a bad or leaky cartridge, but I am happy to just open another because of all the money I am saving. Also, since the generic cartridges are only 99 cents, I don't bother attempting to refill them.

The printer companies will try to tell you that the generic ink might harm your printer. That's ok with me. If my printer does fail after I have used two or more changes of generic ink, I am still ahead. With the money I have saved by using the generic ink, I can buy a new printer and do it again.

The cheapest printer to use is a standard laser printer. Your cost per page will be the lowest. Laser printer and copy machine cartridges can also be refilled with toner. My Xerox XD100 printer/copy machine is on its sixth refill and first drum replacement. I purchased both toner refill and a drum on Ebay. Replacing each took a screwdriver and about 15 minutes of my time. The cost savings in this case was over $300 dollars.

A Frugal purchase is a laser all in one. It will print, copy, scan and fax. It will keep your printing costs low and you can use it to make copies of your rebates.

The next time you buy a printer, research the cost and availability of generic ink and toner. To see a list of low cost ink websites, visit TheFrugalFactor.com.

The Hidden Value

If you have children that need school supplies, save your ink cartridges. Staples provides $3 in rewards for each ink cartridge you turn in. The limit is ten per month, and the money can only be spent at Staples. But, it's still a great deal for something you might normally throw out.

That's $30 per month. If you don't go through 10 cartridges per month team up with a friend or neighbor. Find out what happens to those cartridges at work. If they are being thrown out, start scooping them up.

At the time of this writing, Staples will take ANY ink cartridge. Even generic ink cartridges. The generic cartridges I buy for my printers only cost 99 cents each. So, I could even give them new generic cartridges and be ahead. Office Depot currently provides a ream (that's 500 sheets) of paper for each cartridge you turn in.

7

Ebay

Ebay can be an excellent tool to sell your old technology, free items and excess frugal deals.   Ebay can become an excellent tool in your Frugal lifestyle.

Ebay Factor

Buying items that have discounts, rebates, and coupon codes, is a good way to upgrade your lifestyle. In today's high tech world, it's sometimes better to upgrade sooner than later. Don't keep your digital cameras, computers, MP3 players, and other high tech equipment so long that it's of no use to anyone. Sell your old technology items on Ebay! After the sale of the old technology, and the return of your rebate (from the new item) the new item may be free, or almost FREE.

Another strategy is to sell the bonus item on Ebay. I have sold several printers that came as a free bonus when I purchased a new computer, or digital camera. By selling the printer, I reduced my out-of-pocket cost for the original item.

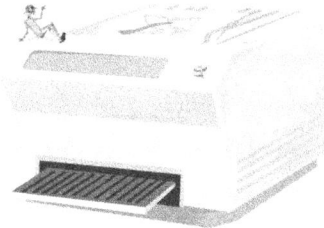

Ebay Profits

At times you will encounter such great deals that you can make a fair amount of money. Selling items on Ebay can be profitable, especially if you have a large quantity of desirable and identical products. Since the products are the same, when one sells you can simply re-list the auction with little effort.

This opportunity has happened to me several times. Radio Shack sold TIVO's for $50 each, and offered a $50 rebate. The rebate had a limit of 10 per address. Also, when the customer activated the TIVO, they would receive a $170 rebate.

It was a Win-Win-Win. I purchased as many Tivo's as I could find. I drove up to two hours away from my house, buying up every TIVO that Radio Shack had. Radio Shack's website showed the location, address and phone number of every store. That information, along with my GPS made the traveling easy.

I used friends and relative's address's to send the rebates in so that I could get more than 10. I had Radio Shack ring up each TIVO separately so I could provide the Ebay customer with the receipt and rebate form for each one.

In the end I purchased over 60 TIVO's with an average selling price of $118. I wasn't able to get the rebates on all of them. They were selling so well on Ebay, the rebate was a nice bonus. You can do the math. This was still a very good deal. I used the profit from this deal to bring my family on a spring break cruise!

Another time, I walked into an Office Depot store with my children. One of my daughters saw a hand written sign on mobile cart that had backpacks on it. The sign said $5. Now these were name brand backpacks, SwissGear and Jansport. The retail price on them ranged from $49 - $69.

My daughter pulled on my hand and said her backpack strap was broken, and asked if I would buy her one. I said "yes, But I don't think they are five dollars." I had her walk over to an employee and ask. I watched as he said "yes, they are five dollars." He looked up at me as I held my hand up with 5 fingers stretched out and he shook his head, "yes".

I let the kids pick one backpack out each. As I started to sort through them I realized I hit the jackpot! I filled a shopping cart and headed to the register. The cashier had to manually mark down each one to $5. Then she also gave me a discount for my Teacher Rewards card! I went to the van and piled the backpacks inside.

My children happily got in the van and buckled their seatbelts. I though for a moment and said, "let's go back in". We went in and filled another shopping cart. It didn't end there. The next week I drove to other stores, asking if they were willing to sell their backpacks for $5. Since the back to school season was, over many managers agreed.

I turned around and listed all of the laptop backpacks on Ebay and made a very good profit. At Christmastime I gave some backpacks to relatives, and the rest went to the Toys for Tots program. These opportunities happen, you just need to keep alert.

Winning the Auction

Have you ever bid on an auction, only to be outbid in the last few moments? If that happened, you have been "Sniped".

A Snipe program is a tool that will bid on your behalf in the last few seconds of an Ebay auction. It's an effective tool that increases your chance of winning the auction at the lowest possible price.

There are many sniping program services on the Internet some are free and others charge a small fee. If you interested in winning your next auction check out these sites:

JustSnipe.com
HammerSnipe.com
Esnipe.com

8

Vacations

Planning a vacation should not be a frustrating task. Using the internet and a few key web sites will help make your next vacation fun and Frugal.

Hotels

Use the internet to find the best hotel for the price. Using TripAdvisor.com makes this an easy task. Before making a reservation visit the hotel's website directly to see if you can get a better deal. Also, call the hotel directly. Don't call the reservation line. Call directly to that specific hotel property. Then make the reservation from the cheapest source.

If there are no cancellation penalties, call the hotel the night before your stay and ask for the best possible rate. Don't tell the operator that you already have a reservation. You may be quoted a much lower rate. Remember, hotel rooms don't bring in any money unless they're used. So, the closer the date, the cheaper the rate.

Finally, when you arrive at the hotel walk in and find out what it costs to spend the night. Sometimes the walk-in rate is even better than your reservation. There have been times that I have walked back to my car called and canceled my reservation because the walk-in rate was cheaper.

When you arrive at the hotel, take a look around at neighboring hotels. If you have time, check out their facilities and room rates. You may find a better deal or nicer place to stay.

With a family of five, I always look for a free continental breakfast. It makes life cheaper, and easier in the morning!

Of course, stay away from any hotels that look like a horror movie was filmed there! The phrase, "You can't tell a book by its cover," doesn't always apply.

For the best hotel rates check these websites:

TripAdvisor.com
TravelZoo.com
OneTravel.com

Vacation Tip

When on vacation bring a disposable camera, or a camera that takes AA batteries. That high tech camera you have won't do you any good if your forgot to charge the batteries or you left the memory card behind. Plus you may visit areas that you don't want to bring your expensive camera, like the beach!

Code 452

Plane Flights

In my experience getting the best deal on a plane flight can be tricky. You can use several websites. But even then you may not get the lowest price, simply because prices are constantly changing. Also some airlines like Southwest are not on the comparison websites. So, you will need to go to Southwest.com to check their prices directly.

After your reservations are made, keep an eye on the prices. If the prices drop, call the airlines and ask them to adjust the cost of your fare.

When flying, if you have a long layover, bring your own snacks. It's nice knowing what you have to snack on before you leave for your trip. If you can not bring liquids on the plane, bring an empty water bottle, so you can fill it from the airport water fountain. It sure beats paying for water and waiting in line.

When looking for the best airline fares check these sites:

Kayak.com
FareCast.com
AirFareWatchDog.com
Qixo.com

For car rentals check:

Breezenet.com
Hotwire.com

9

Other Deals

Black Friday

Black Friday - is the day after Thanksgiving. It's the traditional start of the official Christmas shopping season. On this day, stores have massive discounts on certain items, loss leaders to get you in the door, and lots and lots of rebates. This is the day you've heard about on the news when people line up outside stores in lawn chairs at 2 AM or earlier just to be one of the first ones in.

The "black" in the name comes from the standard accounting practice of using red ink to denote negative values (i.e., losses) and black ink to denote positive values (profits). Black Friday is the day when retailers traditionally get back "in the black" after operating "in the red" for the previous months.

Black Friday Strategy

Equipment needed: sneakers, small binoculars, cell phone, food & drink, friends & family.

1. Get the advertisements from the paper ahead of time. Each year TheFrugalFactor.com provides information on the best places to view the ads before they are published. Be sure to install our toolbar to find the information when it happens. Remember that some newspapers may not have all the ads. So if you have more than one major paper in your area get both!

2. Go through each advertisement page by page. Circle the items you want. Many times, stores offer the exact same items on sale, so compare prices. Use a 3 x 5 card for each store making a list of what you want. Use additional cards to tape the actual advertisement and photo of each product.

   Know the rebates before you get to the store. The night before, many rebates will be online. In some cases you will be able to buy the item online instead of going to the store. These online sales go out of stock early, so you will need to watch the web sites carefully. Also, depending on your time zone, these deals may show up at midnight or 1 AM.

   When it doubt about the rebate buy the quantity you want, and know the store return policy. You can always return the items you do not want.

2. After you have gone through all the advertisements rate the products. Place the items that are most important to you at the top of the stack.

4. On the store card write down the time each store opens.

5. Recruit friends and family! Yes, you will need multiple people for this shopping adventure. Discuss who will go to which store first. Then divide the 3 X 5 cards up. Remember you have pictures taped to the cards, so it will be easy for your crew to located the merchandise.

   If you have children old enough to shop alone for you, that do not have a credit card, drop them at the store and have them gather the merchandise in a cart and wait for you. We did this once, and because of the competition the kid had to hide the "deal merchandise" in a stereo cabinet, because people started shopping out of her cart!

   Discuss which store will be visited first. Have the person who has shopped there the most go to that store. You want someone who knows the layout. I know some shoppers that visit the stores a day or two before Black Friday just to see the placement of products and pallets.

   Place each stores cards in a separate envelope. Put the cards in the car. Only take the cards into the store that you need. Leave the other cards in the car.

6. The day before Black Friday, "Preparation Thursday" get all your materials ready. Clothes, wallet, credit cards, breakfast bars or candy bars. Dress warm, it may be very cold at 1 a.m. or earlier.

7. Hit the most important stores early. I mean early! Some customers will be their 6-12 hours before the opening. You need to decide how important that $300 laptop (or another item is). It can be fun to be in line hours before the opening. It's a real event; some stores have contests while customers wait in line, and give away gift cards, or donuts and juice. Those are the smart stores; they provide good customer service and ensure our return next year. Some stores even hand out maps of the store with the deal items numbered so you know were to go. Most stores hand out vouchers for the deals that are limited in supply. This is done to stop fighting inside the store.

   Remember those binoculars? Use them to get a look inside the stores windows to see the location of your prime targets.

   Note: Don't drink a lot before that morning. Rest rooms are hard to find at 4AM. Hey, people brush your teeth, I might be standing next to you, I would like to talk to you but morning breath in my face I don't need.

8. Speed is king. If it looks right bring a small fold up baby stroller, it easier to move down the isles past other people with full size carts. Think about the size of the items and the layout of the store. If it will fit in one of those hand carry baskets pick one of those up at the store entrance instead of the full size cart.

Tag team the store. If you are lucky enough to have two people per store have one person hold your place in line at the register. Have them hold one item as if they want it. If you're not ready when they get to the front of the line, have them let a few people ahead of them until you're ready. This is the best strategy to get out of the store quickly. Remember to be human, be kind, and use social engineering to get things going your way.

Quickly find all the items you want and head to the register. DO NOT browse. If it was not on your cards, you're not after it. Get what you have on your list and RUN (Ok, walk). Divide the items up at the register into separate piles and have them ring up one set at a time.

You will need separate receipts for each set of rebate items. Each person you will be buying for will need a separate receipt.

9. Be sure to have a separate secure pocket for those receipts. If you lose the receipts, you've lost the rebates!

10. Head to the next store and do it again. Remember, you have the next store's set of cards in the car waiting. Giddy up and go.

11. Meet your Black Friday crew at a local restaurant for lunch and divide up the products and receipts, and share your Black Friday stories.

The Letter

At times it is necessary to make contact with a company. This may be for an issue with a shipment, rebate or warranty. First try and contact them by email if that does not work give them a call.

Your first call will get you to the lowest member of the customer service department, who may not be able to provide you with a solution. Many times you will need to ask for a supervisor to get faster results. Customer service representatives (CSR's) at the lower levels cannot just pass you up the line. You must ask for a supervisor. I have spoken to some CSR's that have told me that they are often hoping the customer on the other end of the phone will ask for a supervisor. Because without doing that, they cannot move you to a higher level, to someone who has the authority to solve your problem.

When these steps fails write a letter to the company. Find the company's headquarters by searching on the internet. Find the name of the CEO, president, or the company's Department of Consumer Affairs. It is unlikely that the CEO of the company will read your letter. But one of their assistants will read the letter, and have the power to solve your problem.

In your letter state the problem and provide specifics of the incident. Include copies of all material and the dates that you called attempting to resolve the issue. Tell them exactly what you want from them to resolve your problem. Let them know what you expect in return. For example: a new product, refund, discount, a free month's service.

Explain in your letter that you will file a report with the FTC and the States Attorney General for your state if there is no response. Request a response within 30 days.

If there is no response send a second letter, and file the complaint with the FTC, and the Attorney General of your state.

Federal Trade Commission (FTC) Online Complaint Form FTC.gov, 877-FTC-HELP (877-382-4357)

National Association of Attorneys General at NAAG.org Find your state attorney general's contact info, and call in a complaint.

You can also post your problem on the following websites:

ConsumerAffairs.com - is a private, non-governmental entity that empowers consumers by providing a forum for their complaints.

PlanetFeedBack.com – helps you write a complaint letter and forward it to the company.

RipOffReport.com – Allows you to share your horror stories with other consumers.

Note: If the problem is with a food product keep the packaging. Code numbers on the packages will help the manufacturer narrow down when the product was produced, and from what factory.

Don't just send complaint letters. Also, send a letter when you are happy about a product or store personnel. Sometimes service is so good, you need to give an employee praise right away and write a letter. This happened when a waiter at a restaurant went the extra mile to keep my children happy. At the time, the kids were still in highchairs and as many of you know, kids can make a real mess. Well, the waiter did an outstanding job. Not just serving but entertaining the children and keeping everyone happy. So when the check came I told the waiter I needed to see the manager. They asked what was wrong, I replied, "I just need to see the manager". It worried the waiter. When the manager arrived the waiter was standing a few feet behind him. I explained to the manager that the waiter was excellent and really kept my family happy, and that I realize that it's not often customers report positive experiences. The manager appreciated the comments and I could see the waiter relief as I spoke to the manager. I also left the waiter a very good tip!

In the future, an unreasonable guest may complain about the same waiter. I hope if that happens, the manager will remember how happy I was with their service.

Cell Phone Secrets

It can be really expensive to replace your broken cell phone. Even if your cell phone provider is willing to give a new phone for free, they will lock you into a two or three year contract.

If you can do without the newest cell phone technology, there is a cheap way to replace your phone.

AT&T, and T-Mobile both have pay-as-you-go cell phone plans. You can go to either of their web sites and get a prepaid phone for under $30, shipped. After you get the phone, all you need to do is put the SIM card from your broken phone, into the new prepaid phone. By doing this you will be using your monthly plan.

At times you can find one of the prepaid phones free after rebate, or a bonus prepaid card included for minutes. If you don't need the prepaid card you can sell it on Ebay for about 90% of its face value.

Be sure to buy a prepaid phone from the same provider that you have your monthly plan. If not the phone will need to be unlocked.

Some brands of phones, especially Nokia, can be unlocked and used on most cell phone services. It's an easy thing to do, and the directions are readily available for most models by searching online. I always search for the unlocking instructions *before* purchasing the phone.

Expense Tracking

Keep track of your monthly expenses, especially the re-occurring ones. Do you pay everyday for morning coffee, lunch, or drinks after work? Figure out what these items cost you every week and multiply by fifty-two. That will give you the figure for the year.

For example:

Coffee at $2 day x 5 = $10
Lunch at $7 a day x 5 = 35
Total $45 week x 52 = **$2,340**

If you save just half that amount by making your own coffee and bringing your lunch to work, at the end of the year you will have enough money to take a nice vacation, pay down a credit card bill, or start an early retirement fund.

Cars

Run your car until it just can't be repaired. Currently all of our cars have over 100,000 miles on them, and I don't expect to replace any of them soon. Repair and upkeep costs have always been less than a monthly payment.

When you drive down the road and see all of those nice new cars, remember that the bank owns most of them not the driver.

Always check the reliability ratings online and in Consumer Reports before purchasing a car.

The Frugal Check List

Below is a simple checklist to start your Frugal Lifestyle.

1. Use your credit card to make all purchases, but pay it off each month. This will allow you to earn cash back, or rewards points.

2. Use the credit card that will provide you the greatest reward for the purchase. Some cards pay a higher rate for gas, restaurants, home improvement, and travel expenses.

3. Open an online savings account. As your Frugal ways provide you with additional money, move it into your online savings account to earn the greatest interest.

4. Force yourself to save by depositing your rebate check in an online savings account.

5. Pay all of your bills using online bill pay. By doing this you save on postage.

6. Set up your bills to be paid online when they arrive in your mailbox. By using online bill pay, you can have the bill paid just before the due date. This will save you from late fees.

7. Raise the deductible on your auto and home insurance. This greatly reduces the cost. Put your savings in a separate account. If you ever have a claim you will have already saved the deductible.

8. Each year, call around to see if you can get better rates on your homeowners and auto insurance. Shop for the lowest rate and best coverage.

9. Eliminate or reduce all unnecessary reoccurring monthly charges or subscription fees, or call to see if you can reduce the cost by changing plans. This includes Cable/Satellite television, cell phone, internet services and more.

10. If you make long distance, overseas phone calls, sign up for a Skype account. Skype is a software application that allows users to make phone calls over the Internet. Calls to other users of the service are free of charge. Calls made to landlines and mobile phones are made for a fee.

11. Cancel your landline phone and use only your cell phone. We have gone for years without a landline phone and have not missed it at all. We have a family cell phone plan and share the minutes. Since most of our family and friends are with the same service provider, we get to talk to them for free.

12. Replace your standard light bulbs with compact fluorescents. The will save you money on your electricity bill. Also, these bulbs can last up to five years, making them perfect for the hard to reach areas of your home. No more getting the ladder out to change bulbs.

13. Protect your electronics with a quality surge suppressors from American Power Conversion or Tripp Lite.

14. Take advantage of free pens and pencils at banks, hotels, and conventions. Now that's cheap!

15. When spending the night at a hotel, pick up those little soaps each day and keep the ones you do not use. At most hotels newly wrapped soaps will appear the next day.

16. If you do stop at a fast food restaurant, don't throw out your extra napkins. Bring them home!

17. Don't throw out your old ink cartridges. Turn them into an office supply store for free paper, or rewards.

18. Buy enough paper and pencils during the back to school sales for the entire year. Office supply stores put great discounts on supplies during their back to school promotions to earn your back to school dollars.

19. Buy your children backpacks or book bags they can use for years. They may think the Spiderman backpack is the best thing in the world right now, but by the time they are seniors in high school it probably won't be cool anymore!

20. Use generic toner or ink in your printer.

21. When printing documents off the internet to read away from the computer, use your printer's draft mode to save ink.

22. Use a laser printer when color is not needed. Laser printers are much cheaper to operate than a color inkjet.

23. Use your printer to print your own birthday cards.

24. Bring your lunch to work.

25. Have coffee and breakfast at home before leaving work.

26. Cook at home instead of eating out.

27. Actually use the leftovers in your refrigerator. Don't let them become science experiments!

28. In the winter, when you are done cooking in the oven, shut it off and open the door a little. This will allow the unused heat, to heat your home.

29. Drink water, not soda.

30. Rinse and reuse water bottles.

31. Buy a reverse osmosis water system on Ebay and bottle your own water. Installing a reverse osmosis system is any easy do it yourself project.

32. Eat before grocery shopping.

33. Create a Frugal Attack Plan before leaving your house. This includes making a shopping list, gathering all of the coupons for the items on the list, and determining which stores you will visit.

34. When shopping, leave children at home. This will save you money and time.

35. Use a calculator when shopping. The calculator can be used not just to keep and eye on your total, but also to compare the

cost of items. Use the calculator to discover the cost per ounce, or per item in the package.

36. Build up a stockpile of frugal deals.

37. Cut dryer sheets in half, or use them more than one time.

38. Turn lights off when not in use.

39. Keep the door shut to keep the heat or air conditioning in. If you have children, install spring hinges so the exterior doors shut themselves.

40. Put empty two-liter bottles in the empty space of your freezer. This will insulate the freezer when it's opened and closed by keeping the cold air in.

41. Put cooking oil in a spray bottle instead of buying non-stick spray.

42. Run your dishwasher only when it's full.

43. Rent a carpet machine and clean the rug yourself.

44. Turn off the water while brushing your teeth or shaving.

45. Put a full two-liter bottle in your toilet tank. This will cause the toilet to use less water per flush.

46. Squeeze the old small bars of soap together with the new bar.

47. Use soap that you kept from your last hotel stay.

48. Add water to shampoo to get more uses.

49. Use less detergent when washing clothes.

50. Avoid buying clothes that need dry cleaning.

51. Buy clothes off-season.

52. Buy bread from bakery outlet stores or dollar stores.

53. Buy for next year during after-holiday sales.

54. Salvage your old sofa. If the frame is in good condition, get a slipcover to give it new life.

55. Shop for furniture at estate and garage sales. Also, check Craigslist.

56. Use your children's artwork to decorate your home.

57. Buy durable quality items and take care of them. Use consumer review sites to select the top products in their class.

58. Shop around for prescription drugs. Check Costco, Sam's Club, Target and Wal-Mart. You do not need to be a member to get your prescriptions filled at one of the warehouse clubs.

59. Ask your doctor to write a three-month prescription. Then you will only need to pay the co-pay once every three months.

60. Get your pets shots done at a pet store or local shelter.

61. Change your AC/furnace filter.

62. Install a programmable thermostat.

63. Caulk and insulate your home.

64. Call your power company for a free energy audit. They will look over your home and tell you were you can save money by saving energy.

65. Fix your own appliances. Find the model number and do a search on the internet. You can usually find the part you need complete with instructions on the replacement.

66. Borrow books and movies from the library to save on rental fees.

67. Go to matinee or dollar movie theaters.

68. Buy snacks at the store before going to the movies.

69. Stop smoking. Difficult but profitable.

70. Stop drinking alcoholic beverages.

71. Brush and floss to save on dental bills.

72. Eat right and exercise to save on future medical bills.

73. Buy home a gym. Save on membership, and there is no excuse if it's right in your home.

74. Repair your car instead of buying a new one.

75. Wash and vacuum your car at home.

76. Change your car's air filter.

77. Keep your tires properly inflated.

78. Rotate your tires every 7,000 miles.

79. Shop around for a tire store that provides free balancing and rotation. Most offer free rotation, but there are a few national chains that also provide free balancing.

Code 886

Abbreviations & Acronyms

Below is a list of common terms used on coupon and hot deal forums.

AC – After Coupon.

AR – After rebate.

AYOR – At your own risk.

B&M – Brick and Motar, a physical store's location.

B1G1 or BOGO – Buy one get one free.

Blinkie – Store coupon from a dispenser with a blinking light.

BOLO – Be on the lookout.

BTW – By the way.

CAT – (Catilina) Coupon dispensed at the register after purchase.

CO – Cents off coupon.

CRT – Cash register tape.

CYE – Check your email.

DD – Dumpster dive.

DH – Dear husband.

DND – Did not double.

DW – Dear wife.

ECB – Extra Care Bucks.

FAC – Free after coupon.

FAR – Free after rebate.

HTH – Hope this helps.

IME – In my experience.

IMHO – In my humble opinion.

IP – Internet printable coupon.

ISO – In search of.

KWIM – Know what I mean.

LMK – Let me know.

MIR – Mail in rebate.

MM – Money Maker.

MQ – Manufacturer's coupon.

NED – No expiration date.

OOP – Out of pocket.

OOS – Out of stock

OP – Original poster.

OT – Off topic.

Overage – When you make a purchase with a coupon that exceeds the items cost. The additional amount is put towards other items in your order.

Peelie – A coupon that you peel off the package.

PITA – Pain in the posterior end.

POP – Proof of purchase.

RC – Rain check.

RP – Red Plum supplement coupon insert.

SASE – Self addressed stamped envelope.

SS – Smart Source supplement coupon insert.

Stacking – The use of more than one coupon on an item.

Tearpad – A pad of coupons or rebate forms found hanging on a store shelf or display.

TYVM – Thank you very much.

WSL – While supplies last.

WYB – When you buy.

YMMV – Your mileage may vary. Your success may vary.

YVW – You're very welcome.

Pay it Forward

If you have an extra coupon that you will not use, pass it along to someone in the store. I always look for someone that can use the coupon, a family with small children or mom pushing a stroller, can always use a little extra help. Most of the time the coupon is cheerfully accepted, but sometimes people are very cautious (as I always am) when a stanger approaches them. After they discover your not trying to sell them something, or cause them harm, they usually lighten up.

At a local buffet restaurant I handed the husband and wife behind us in line a Buy One Get One Free coupon. During our dinner the wife approached me and said, "Thank-You, That coupon was great. It saved us almost $10". I told her that the only time we ate there was when I had a coupon!

Spread the joy of the Frugal Factor!

Final Thoughts

Some stores have excellent rebates and coupon policies. Others do not! Remember that the only constant in life is change. Some stores that had excellent rebates a year ago, no longer have any rebate items.

Stores and store managers are very different. If you do not have success at one store, try another store. I have found that managers at the same retail store differ greatly.

Always be kind and polite. Remember these stores and employees are only trying to do their jobs as they have been trained. Poor employee training and customer service is something we need to deal with while smiling. You won't always win at the Frugal Factor game. But as your skills and resources grow so, will your savings and profitability.

Always support the employees and stores that are Frugal Friendly. Report them to TheFrugalFactor.com and we will add them to our Frugal Friendly list.

Even though you have reached the last page of the book, the story is not over. To continue your Frugal adventure with us go to:

TheFrugalFactor.com

A

Abbreviations · 7, 127
Address · 16, 17, 19, 27, 37, 54, 86, 99
AirFareWatchDog.com · 106
Amazon.com · 27, 47, 48
American Express · 2, 83, 86
American Power Conversion · 119
Annual fee · 83, 86
AnnualCreditReport.com · 90
Apple · 36
Appliances · 48, 124
Applications · 92
AT&T · 116
Attorney General · 114

B

Backpack · 43, 100, 120
Balance transfer · 86
Best Buy · 37, 38, 42, 43
Binder · 21, 45, 65, 80
Black Friday · 7, 19, 108, 109, 110, 111, 112
BOGO · 63, 127
Breakage · 11
Breakfast · 104, 111, 121
Breezenet.com · 106
Brick and motar · 39
Bricks coupons · 70
Brother · 19
Buy and Return · 42

C

Calculator · 68, 121
Call · 124
Cameras · 16, 65, 98
Car Rental · 87
Cars · 7, 117
Cash Advances · 86
Cashier · 6, 65
Cell phone · 109
Centurion Card · 86
CEO · 113
Cereal · 69, 73
Chairs · 19, 108, 115
Chase · 82, 84
Circuit City · 38
Citibank · 82, 88
Comparison-shopping · 29
Competition · 6, 60, 68
CompUSA · 33
Computer · 3, 11, 16, 33, 39, 43, 44, 47, 66, 70, 77, 94, 98, 120
Consumer · 50, 51, 75, 117, 123
ConsumerAffairs.com · 114
ConsumerSearch.com · 48
Costco · 44, 52, 64, 123
Coupon · 6, 56, 62, 70, 75, 80
Coupon binder · 45
CouponCabin.com · 32
CouponMom.com · 70
Coupons.com · 70
Crazy · 8, 65, 67, 80
Credit Cards · 6, 81
CSR · 22, 49, 50, 113
CurrentCodes.com · 32

K

Kayak.com · 106
Kohls · 44

L

L.L. Bean · 44
Laptop · 42, 43
Laser printer · 95, 120
Laundry · 69
Letter · 7, 113
Leverage · 89
Linens & Things · 21
Lowes · 60, 86
Loyalty Cards · 6, 71

M

M&M's · 2, 67
Manager · 45, 50, 52, 61, 62, 67, 115
Manufacturers · 56, 128
MasterCard · 82
Merchant · 88, 89
Milk · 36, 57
Movie · 104, 124
MP3 · 36, 98

N

NAAG.org · 114
NaughtyCodes.com · 32
Newegg.com · 47, 48
Nokia · 116

O

Office Depot · 25, 26, 30, 37, 38, 100
Office supply · 26, 33, 120
Officemax · 19
OneTravel.com · 105
Online Deals · 5, 29
OnRebate · 27
Osmosis · 121
Overage · 129

P

Parago · 27, 28
Paypal · 19, 23
Pencil · 18
Pepsi · 66, 74
Perception · 13
Pharmacy · 6, 64
Post · 56
Price adjustment · 38, 42, 43, 49, 50
Price match · 38, 39, 49, 50, 51, 55, 85
Printer · 7, 13, 93, 94
Proctor and Gamble · 11
Profitable · 9, 56, 81, 99, 124
Purchase protection · 87

Q

Qixo.com · 106

R

Radio Shack · 99
RainChecks · 79
Razors · 69
Rebate · 5, 18, 22, 26, 85

www.ingramcontent.com/pod-product-compliance
Lightning Source LLC
Chambersburg PA
CBHW060611200326
41521CB00007B/741